Giant Cheeseheads!

The Giant-Packer rivalry and the former Giants
who helped the Packers become champions.

Table of Contents

To Sue for all the love, confidence and support that you have given me. Without you, there would be no Giant Cheeseheads!!

New York to Wisconsin....

Growing-up watching Y.A. Tittle pass a football was a beautiful sight. His charge back into the pocket and his pronounced hop are the two images I have of him as he tossed the football all around Yankee Stadium to the likes of Gifford, Shofner, Rote and Morrison. These New York *Football* Giants backed-up their aerial assaults with a bruising defense led by Huff, Robustelli and Grier. With Tittle setting records for TD passes, it was a terrific time to be a Giant fan!

But the Giants lost both the 1961 and 1962 championship games to the Green Bay Packers. Their offense was shut out in both games. Since I was 8 years old at the time, I couldn't understand how a team from Green Bay could beat a team from New York. Not once, but twice. I couldn't even find Green Bay on a map!

After moving to Wisconsin, I eventually "found" Green Bay! I finally became a Packer fan in 1989 and, when I looked back at the 1961 and 1962 title games, I noticed that several legendary Packers had previously been with the New York Giants. After looking at all of the transactions between the teams, the Packers, more often than not, have beaten the Giants both on and off the field! Throughout their history, transactions with the Giants have led the Packers to victories! Giant Cheeseheads looks at the rivalry between these two outstanding franchises and how those who went from New York to Green Bay helped lead the Packers to greatness!

J. R.
July 2012

Giant Cheeseheads!

Giant Cheeseheads are players and coaches who were associated with the Giants before coming to the Packers. They came to Green Bay after either playing for the Giants, coaching in New York or through a special connection between the Giants and the Packers. For the Packers, the magnitude of these transactions cannot be overstated. These former Giants – Giant Cheeseheads – often led the way for Green Bay.

Acquired thru trades, the draft, waivers or free agency

Lionel Aldridge	Ray Nitschke *
Don Chandler	Charlie Peprah
Rudy Comstock	Dick Stahlman
Ryan Grant	Emlen Tunnell *
Cal Hubbard *	"Mule" Wilson
Chuck Mercein	Frank Winters
	Willie Wood *

Giant players/coaches who became Packer coaches

Bill Austin
Vince Lombardi *
Jimmy Robinson
Bob Schnelker
Ray Wietecha

Special Giant-Packer Connections

Arnie Herber *
Clark Hinkle *
Tom Landry *
John "Bo" Molenda
Richard "Red" Smith

* Member of the Pro Football Hall of Fame

The Rivalry!

The Packers and the Giants were members of the National Football League for a few years before they actually faced one another. When the Giants won the championship in 1927 – the Packers finished second – the time had come for their first meeting. Since 1928, the Giants and the Packers have met 57 times including five NFL Championship games. In 2007 and 2011, the rivalry has been rekindled with two postseason victories by the Giants in Green Bay.

But back in 1928…

October 7, 1928

GIANTS 6   PACKERS 0
City Stadium, Green Bay, WI

Running back "Mule" Wilson sets up the game's only score for the Giants. The New York Times reported "…(Cal) Hubbard, Wilson and Caldwell played brilliantly for the Giants…" *Hubbard and Wilson were eventually traded to the Packers and they became key pieces in Green Bay's three-peat from 1929 – 1931.*

November 18, 1928

PACKERS 7   GIANTS 0
Polo Grounds, New York, NY

Kicking played a huge role in this rematch. A blocked punt led to the only score, and Verne Lewellen's punts kept the Giants in their own territory most of the game. *Green Bay's first win over the Giants ends New York's hopes of repeating as NFL champions in 1928.* Let the rivalry begin!

November 24, 1929

PACKERS 20 GIANTS 6
Polo Grounds, New York, NY

"In the brief history of the league, there had never been a game as glamorous as the upcoming collision of these two titans."

With the country reeling from the Stock Market Crash, this game was, in many ways, the NFL's first Super Bowl. *It featured two undefeated teams with the winner likely emerging at season's end as the champion.*

The Packers got off to a fast start in the rain. The favored Giants fumbled on their first possession, and Johnny Blood recovered for Green Bay. The Packers scored a few plays later. The Giants made it 7-6 in the third quarter when quarterback Benny Friedman turned a fake punt into a 38 yard touchdown pass.

But, "Iron Mike" Michalske and Cal Hubbard kept the pressure on Friedman. Occasionally, Packers' Coach Curly Lambeau moved "…big Cal Hubbard out of the line and let him roam around behind it…...to spot and bump any receivers coming through and to plug up whatever holes might open." The strategy helped slow down the Giants.

An impressive fourth quarter put the game away for the Packers. Bo Molenda's touchdown was soon followed by the Johnny "Blood" McNally's score. When Blood scored the final points of the game, he yelled to his teammates *"Let's make 'em like it!" His boastful remark helped stoke the rivalry early on. When the season ended two weeks later, this win was the difference for the Packers. Green Bay shattered the myth that an old town team couldn't compete with teams from the big city.*

Packers	7	0	0	13	20
Giants	0	0	6	0	6

GB   Lewellen 3yd pass to McCreay (Molenda kick)
NY   Friedman 38yd pass to Plansky (kick failed)
GB   Molenda 1yd run (Molenda kick)
GB   Blood 5yd run (Molenda kick)

1929 NFL Standings

	W	L	T	Pct
Green Bay Packers	*12*	*0*	*1*	*1.000*
New York Giants	*13*	*1*	*1*	*.929*
Frankford Yellow Jackets	9	4	5	.692
Chicago Cardinals	6	6	1	.500
Boston Bulldogs	4	4	0	.500
Orange Tornadoes	3	4	4	.429
Staten Island Stapletons	3	4	3	.429
Providence Steam Roller	4	6	2	.400
Chicago Bears	4	9	2	.308
Buffalo Bisons	1	7	1	.125
Minneapolis Red Jackets	1	9	0	.100
Dayton Triangles	0	6	0	.000

Cal Hubbard   *1929-1933, 1935*
The Enforcer

Cal Hubbard was one of the greatest sportsmen of the 20th century. At 6'5" and 250 pounds, he was also one of the largest and most feared players of his time. He was an overpowering lineman both on offense and defense, a one man wrecking crew known to run the 100 yard dash in just over 11 seconds!

In New York, Hubbard teamed with the great Steve Owen

to bring the Giants their first championship in 1927. *After the 1928 season, Hubbard asked to be traded to Green Bay, preferring small towns to big cities. The Giants regretfully accommodated.*

Hubbard had a Hall of Fame career with Green Bay from 1929-1935. He was All-NFL five times, and he was a key member of the Packers' three-peat of 1929 -1931. In 1969, Hubbard was voted one of the NFL's best tackles in its first 50 years. After retiring from football, Hubbard became a standout American League Umpire from 1936-1951. He was eventually named the Supervisor of Umpires in the American League. Today, *Hubbard is still the only person ever inducted into both the Football and Baseball Halls of Fame!*

November 23, 1930

PACKERS 6   GIANTS 13
Polo Grounds, New York, NY

For Green Bay, ten players did not return from the 1929 championship team. The Packers' dominant defense wasn't as strong, but the offense was a powerhouse. *Green Bay extended its undefeated streak to 23 games (two ties included) before losing two games on the road. The second loss was to the Giants.*

The Giants and Packers split their two games in 1930. In October, Green Bay won 14-7 on a spectacular 55 yard, fourth quarter touchdown pass from Red Dunn to Johnny Blood. After the game, Giant quarterback Benny Friedman even admitted that the Giants "…had no problem with anyone else, but the Packers were special. They were so big, and yet they were so fast, that they almost won their games before they took the field."

But the Giants won the rematch in November with Friedman scoring both through the air and on the ground. The Packers, however, did not go down easily. During a late fourth quarter drive to tie the game, Green Bay was penalized three times. A Packer touchdown was also called back due to offsetting penalties!

The Giants' 13-6 win wouldn't be enough, however, to overcome Green Bay's lead in the standings. After the triumph, the Giants went 2-2 the rest of the way while the Packers went 2-1-1. *Green Bay's tie with Portsmouth in the last game of the season gave them a .004 advantage over the Giants and their second straight title.*

Packers	0	0	6	0	6
Giants	0	7	6	0	13

NY   Friedman 22d pass to Badgro (Friedman kick)
NY   Friedman 3yd run (kick failed)
GB   Lewellen, 4yd run (kick failed)

1930 NFL Standings

	W	L	T	Pct
Green Bay Packers	**10**	**3**	**1**	**.769**
New York Giants	**10**	**4**	**0**	**.765**
Chicago Bears	9	4	1	.692
Brooklyn Dodgers	7	4	1	.636
Providence Rollers	6	4	1	.600
Staten Island Stapletons	5	5	2	.500
Chicago Cardinals	5	6	2	.455
Portsmouth Spartans	5	6	3	.455
Frankford Yellow Jackets	4	13	1	.222
Minneapolis Red Jacket	1	7	1	.125
Newark Tornadoes	1	10	1	.091

John Molenda   *1928-32, 1947-48*
Bo

Bo Molenda played and coached for both New York and Green Bay. He was a fine fullback on the great Packer championship teams of 1929-31. He led the Packers in rushing twice, and *his trade to the Giants is still considered one of the more questionable trades in the early history of the Packers.*

After retiring as a player in New York, he stayed on as an assistant coach with Steve Owen and the Giants. When Owen's mother became ill, Bo coached the Giants against the Packers in the 1939 NFL title game! In 1947, he came back to Green Bay to be Curly Lambeau's backfield coach.

November 22, 1931

PACKERS 14 GIANTS 10
Polo Grounds, New York, NY

To strengthen their offensive line before the season, the Packers acquired Dick Stahlman and Rudy Comstock from the Giants. It worked! The Packer offense was so dominant in 1931 that they outscored opponents 291 to 87. They scored 44 touchdowns, which set a franchise record that stood until 1961 when the NFL added two more games to the league schedule.

For the Giants, 1931 was a down year. The Packers beat them twice. In the first game in October, Red Flaherty got the Giants off to a great start by blocking a punt and returning it for a touchdown. The Packers then scored the next 27 points to win easily 27-7.

In November, Johnny Blood scored on the Packers first possession. The Giants came back strong in the second quarter on Benny Friedman's passing and Hap Moran's running and kicking. Moran, a New York native, scored all of the Giants' points.

The Packers won the game in the fourth quarter on a touchdown pass from Red Dunn to rookie back Hank Bruder. *It was an especially sweet victory for several Giant Cheeseheads as "Mule Wilson, Rudy Comstock, Cal Hubbard and Dick Stahlman made Doc March sorry he ever released them and a couple of them told him so during that thrilling fourth quarter."* March was the Giants' secretary/general manager.

The 1929-1931 Packers became the first team in NFL history to win three straight championships. Thirty-six years later, the 1965-1967 Packers would become the second.

Packers	7	0	0	7	14
Giants	0	10	0	0	10

GB Blood 50yd pass from Dunn (Dunn kick)
NY Moran 3yd run (Moran kick)
NY Moran 22yd FG
GB Bruder 20yd pass from Dunn (Dunn kick)

1931 NFL Standings

	W	L	T	Pct
Green Bay Packers	*12*	*2*	*0*	*.857*
Portsmouth Spartans	11	3	0	.786
Chicago Bears	8	5	0	.615
Chicago Cardinals	5	4	0	.556
New York Giants	*7*	*6*	*1*	*.538*
Providence St. Rollers	4	4	3	.500
Staten Island Stapletons	4	6	1	.400
Cleveland Indians	2	8	0	.200
Brooklyn Dodgers	2	12	0	.143
Frankford Yellow Jackets	1	6	1	.143

The Modern NFL

The 1932 season ended in controversy. At the time, the NFL *did not* count tie games in the standings. Ties were treated as if the game had not been played. As a result, the final standings for 1932 were…

	W	L	T	Pct.
* Chicago	7	1	6	.875
Packers	10	3	1	.769
* Portsmouth	6	2	4	.750

 * Chicago and Portsmouth ended their seasons 6-1. The Bears won the playoff game. This win was added to the final standings even though it was played indoors (due to snow) and on a field that was only 80 yards long!

How the final standings would look today…

	W	L	T	Pct.
Packers	10	3	1	.750
Portsmouth	6	1	4	.727
Chicago	6	1	6	.692

"We really won four (championships) in a row, but they didn't give it to us," bemoaned Cal Hubbard. Though the Bears won by the rules, the Packers felt cheated. They had won four more games than the Bears in 1932 and the Packers were 1-1-1 against them during the season. In 1933, partly because of this controversial finish, teams were split into two divisions with division winners playing for the championship.

Eastern Division	**Western Division**
Boston Redskins	Chicago Bears
Brooklyn Dodgers	Chicago Cardinals
New York Giants	Cincinnati Reds
Philadelphia Eagles	Green Bay Packers
Pittsburgh Pirates	Portsmouth Spartans

December 13, 1936
NFL Championship Game

PACKERS 21 REDSKINS 6
Polo Grounds, New York, NY

New York Daily News Reporter Jack Miley called the Green Bay Packers…the finest pro footballers in these United States…

The Packers won their first NFL championship game *in New York but against the Boston Redskins!* The game was played in New York because of poor attendance for the Redskins in Boston. The following year, the Redskins relocated to Washington, D.C.

Prior to the game, the Packers were hailed as the "greatest forward passing team that ever invaded New York." They did not disappoint. The first time they had the ball, quarterback Arnie Herber connected with Don Hutson for a 43 yard touchdown pass. The Redskins fought from behind all game, but an injury to their Hall of Fame running back Cliff Battles severely limited their offense. In the third quarter, after a long completion to Johnny Blood, Herber threw a short touchdown pass to make it 14-6. The Packers held the Redskins scoreless in the second half to win the title!

Packers	7	0	7	7	21
Redskins	0	6	0	0	6

GB   Hutson 43yd pass from Herber (Smith kick)
Bos Rentner 1yd run (Kick failed)
GB   Gantenbein 8yd pass from Herber (Smith kick)
GB   Monnett 2yd run (Engebretsen kick)

```
┌─────────────────────────────────────────┐
│          1936 NFL Standings               │
│                                           │
│  Eastern Division      W  L  T   Pct      │
│  Boston Redskins       7  5  0   .583     │
│  Pittsburgh Pirates    6  6  0   .500     │
│  New York Giants       5  6  1   .455     │
│  Brooklyn Dodgers      3  8  1   .273     │
│  Philadelphia Eagles   1 11  0   .083     │
│                                           │
│  Western Division      W  L  T   Pct      │
│  Green Bay Packers    10  1  1   .909     │
│  Chicago Bears         9  3  0   .750     │
│  Detroit Lions         8  4  0   .667     │
│  Chicago Cardinals     3  8  1   .273     │
└─────────────────────────────────────────┘
```

December 11, 1938
NFL Championship Game

PACKERS   17   GIANTS   23
Polo Grounds, New York, NY

This was a struggle of such magnificent stature that words seem such feeble tools for describing it.

Three weeks before this championship game, the Giants had beaten the Packers 15-3. The rematch would be remembered as a fierce battle that injured three of the game's best players - Don Hutson of the Packers and Mel Hein and Ward Cuff of the Giants.

The Giants blocked two punts and got out to an early 9-0 lead. But Arnie Herber and Clarke Hinkle led Green Bay's comeback that narrowed the Giants' lead to 16-14 at half. In the third quarter, quarterback Ed Danowski engineered a legendary 62 yard drive that put the Giants ahead to stay. The winning score came on a pass from Danowski to

Hank Soar, another future American League Umpire! Though the Packers threatened in the fourth quarter, they could not score. The New York Daily News summed up the action with "… the Giants struck fast, built up an early lead, lost it, and surged back through the gathering shadows for a sensational touchdown – and victory!"

After the game, Curly Lambeau blasted the officiating. But it was his own ineptitude that likely cost the Packers the game. On his way to the locker room at halftime, he got lost and locked out of the Polo Grounds! By the time he got back into the stadium, halftime was ending. New York went on to hold the Packers to just three points in the second half.

Packers	0	14	3	0	17
Giants	9	7	7	0	23

NY Cuff 13yd FG
NY Leemans 6yd run (kick fails)
GB Mulleneaux 50yd pass from Herber (Engebretsen kick)
NY Barnard 20yd pass from Danowski (Cuff kick)
GB Hinkle 6yd run (Engebretsen kick)
GB Engebretsen 15yd FG
NY Soar 23yd pass from Danowski (Cuff kick)

1938 NFL Standings

Eastern Division	W	L	T	Pct
New York Giants	*8*	*2*	*1*	*.800*
Washington Redskins	6	3	2	.667
Brooklyn Dodgers	4	4	3	.500
Philadelphia Eagless	5	6	0	.455
Pittsburgh Pirates	2	9	0	.182

Western Division	W	L	T	Pct
Green Bay Packers	*8*	*3*	*0*	*.727*
Detroit Lions	7	4	0	.636
Chicago Bears	6	5	0	.545
Cleveland Rams	4	7	0	.364
Chicago Cardinals	2	9	0	.182

Clarke Hinkle *1932-41*
RB – LB – DB

Clarke Hinkle is perhaps "…the finest all-around player in Packer history." At 5' 11" and 207 pounds, his talent, versatility and toughness put him among Green Bay's best all-time in rushing, field goals, punting and interceptions.

Hinkle might have put up those numbers for the Giants had Green Bay not signed him right out from under the recruiting eye of the Giants! As an All-American running back from Bucknell in 1931, Hinkle was recruited heavily by the Giants. They invited him and his college coach to sit on the Giants' bench during the Green Bay game on November 22. He took the Giants up on the offer but, during the second half, he went over to the Packers' side of the field. *He came away so impressed with the Packers – especially with Cal Hubbard – that he eventually chose Green Bay over New York for his Hall of Fame career!*

Hinkle's ten years were nothing short of spectacular on both offense and defense. When he retired in 1941, Hinkle was the NFL's all-time leading rusher. He was one of the hardest hitting players in NFL history and fast enough to cover receivers. His physical confrontations with Bronco Nagurski of the Bears are legendary.

From 1936-39, Hinkle, Herber and Hutson led Green Bay to three NFL championship games. The Packers won two, going 1-1 against the Giants. Hinkle is a member of the Pro Football Hall of Fame and the Packers' outdoor practice field is named in his honor.

December 10, 1939
NFL Championship Game

GIANTS 0   PACKERS 27
State Fair Park, West Allis, WI

If we had to lose, there is no team I would rather lose to…
                              Tim Mara, Owner, NY Giants

This was a match-up between NFL champions from 1936
and 1938. To generate more ticket sales and revenue,
the game was played near Milwaukee rather than in
Green Bay. The teams still battled 35 mph winds that
even rattled the park's old press box!

*This was a payback game for the Packers who had lost
the title game to the Giants in 1938.* They exacted their
revenge by scoring nearly every time they had the ball.
Cecil Isbell's 31 yard touchdown pass to veteran Joe
Laws was the play of the day. The Packers also controlled
the game defensively with four interceptions.

*"The Packers were the better team out there today…we
were just outplayed…" said Giant Assistant Coach Bo
Molenda* who coached the Giants in the absence of
Steve Owen. Green Bay held the Giants to 164 total yards
and "…poured pure football onto an arch enemy which
had dealt it a death blow in the 1938 playoff…".

*Green Bay dominated New York and recorded the first
shutout in championship game history.*

IIIII
TEAM OF THE DECADE
Green Bay Packers
NFL CHAMPIONS
1930, 1931, 1936, 1939

Giants	0	0	0	0	0
Packers	7	0	10	10	27

GB Herber 7yd pass to Gantenbein (Gantenbein kick)
GB Engebretsen 29yd FG
GB Isbell 31yd pass to Laws (Engebretsen kick)
GB Smith 42yd FG
GB Jankowski 1yd run (Smith kick

1939 NFL Standings

Eastern Division	W	L	T	Pct
New York Giants	*9*	*1*	*1*	*.900*
Boston Redskins	8	2	1	.800
Brooklyn Dodgers	4	6	1	.400
Philadelphia Eagles	1	9	1	.100
Pittsburgh Pirates	1	9	1	.100

Western Division	W	L	T	Pct
Green Bay Packers	*9*	*2*	*0*	*.818*
Chicago Bears	8	3	0	.727
Detroit Lions	6	5	0	.545
Cleveland Rams	5	5	1	.500
Chicago Cardinals	1	10	1	.091

December 11, 1939
Green Bay Press Gazette Headline

Move Green Bay Franchise?
No! Says Mara; Halas Echoes

New York and Bears Will Stand
Behind Packers for Keeps

Arnie Herber   _1930-40_
Flash

Arnie Herber was pro football's first great _long_ passer.
His long, arcing throws were like a "Ruthian home run."
From 1935-1940, he teamed with Don Hutson to become
one of the game's first great passing combinations.
Herber led the NFL in passing and touchdowns three
times while bringing his hometown Packers two titles
in 1936 and 1939. The Herber to Hutson connection
helped transform pro football from a running game to
a wide-open passing game.

_After retiring from the Packers in 1940, Herber returned
in 1944 to lead the Giants._ He came out of retirement
for his old assistant coach, Red Smith, who was now
an assistant with the Giants. _He brought the Giants
to the title game in 1944 where they lost to the Packers._

December 17, 1944
NFL Championship Game

PACKERS   14   GIANTS   7
Polo Grounds, New York, NY

World War II had the nation's full attention in 1944 and
over 600 active NFL players served in the armed forces.
Former players came out of retirement to fill the void, but
the quality of play was not as strong.

To win their sixth championship, the Packers would face
the daunting task of defeating a former coach and a former
quarterback on the road. _They would also have to reverse
a bitter defeat to the Giants in November when Curly
Lambeau had accused former Packer assistant coach
Red Smith – now with the Giants – of spying on Packer
practices near West Point, NY._

Ted Fritsch, Wisconsin's own, was the hero. He scored all of Green Bay's points in the second quarter. First, he scored on a short run; later on one of only 11 passes thrown by the Packers all game. On the touchdown pass, the Giants triple-teamed Don Hutson, which left Fritsch wide open. Even the New York Times noted that Hutson's "…brilliant fakery made the touchdown possible."

With their league-leading rusher, Bill Paschal, out for most of the game, the Giants didn't score until Ward Cuff's touchdown in the fourth quarter. But three interceptions by Joe Laws against his old teammate – Arnie Herber – stymied the Giant offense. *Herber kept New York's title hopes alive right down to the last possession before finally falling to his former team.* Herber would play one more year for the Giants before ending his Hall of Fame career.

Packers	0	14	0	0	14
Giants	0	0	0	7	7

GB Fritsch 2yd run (Hutson kick)
GB Comp 28yd pass to Fritsch (Hutson kick)
NY Cuff 1yd run (Strong kick)

1944 NFL Standings

Eastern Division	W	L	T	Pct
New York Giants	*8*	*1*	*1*	*.889*
Philadelphia Eagles	7	1	2	.875
Wash. Redskins	6	3	1	.800
Boston Yanks	2	8	0	.200
Brooklyn Tigers	0	10	0	.000

Western Division	W	L	T	Pct
Green Bay Packers	*8*	*2*	*0*	*.800*
Chicago Bears	6	3	1	.667
Detroit Lions	6	3	1	.667
Cleveland Rams	4	6	0	.400
Card-Pitt Carpets	0	10	0	.000

Richard Smith _1927, 1929, 1936-43_
Red

Red Smith also played and coached for both Green Bay and New York. He was Curly Lambeau's only assistant coach for eight seasons but_, after a dispute with Lambeau in 1944, Smith left for the Giants._

After the Giants defeated the Packers in November, Lambeau accused Smith of spying on Packer practices before the game. He claimed that the Giants were "in all the right places at all the right times" even on several new plays and formations. Accusations flew back and forth in newspapers in both New York and Green Bay. Though spying was never proven, passing along information about the Packers to the Giants was something that Smith or any football coach would have done.

NFL Titles

Vince Lombardi   _1959-67_

After a disastrous 1958 season, it had been more than a decade since Green Bay celebrated a winning season much less a championship. Its location, outdated facilities and poor play made it the joke of the league – Siberia – some called it.

The construction of City Stadium in 1957 (now Lambeau Field) addressed the facilities concern. _Now determined to improve on the field in 1959, the Packers hired New York Giants Assistant Coach Vince Lombardi._ They gave Lombardi a five year contract and complete control of the franchise.   He moved quickly to build a more professional and disciplined organization. To do so, he demanded perfection in order to reach excellence. Along the way, he also changed the uniforms!

Lombardi's knowledge, energy and presence instilled respect and accountability. To change the Packers from losers to winners, Lombardi brought along several indispensable players, coaches and approaches from the New York Giants.

Emlen Tunnell   _1959-61_

An all-pro defensive back with the Giants for ten years, Lombardi wanted Tunnell's leadership with the 4-3 defense that he was bringing from the Giants. In 1959, Tunnell was an all-pro in Green Bay, and he helped the Packers understand Lombardi's temperament and his approach to football. _He mentored both Willie Wood and Herb Adderley._ He is still second in the NFL for all-time interceptions (79), and he was the first black player inducted into the Pro Football Hall of Fame in 1967. Both Wood and Adderley joined him there in the 1980s.

Bill Austin *1959-64*

A fine offensive guard for the Giants for nine years, Austin coached the Packers' offensive line from 1959–1964. He was instrumental in the success of Green Bay's power sweep.

Lombardi's Locker Room Sign, 1962

<u>**Home of the Green Bay Packers**</u>
The Yankees of Football

Lombardi brought his New York Giant offense to Green Bay. Conerly, Gifford and Webster were upgraded to Starr, Hornung and Taylor. He believed that basic blocking and tackling – done better than anyone else – was the key to success. Packer opponents frequently knew what play was coming, but they still had trouble stopping it because of near perfect execution.

The power sweep and the half back option were staples of Green Bay's new offense. The results were dramatic. A first game win over the Bears heralded the team's 7-5 finish. In Lombardi's second year, the Packers were in the NFL Championship Game. In his third season, Green Bay won it all by defeating Lombardi's old Giants 37-0!

Playing the Giants was always special for Lombardi. It gave him the opportunity to go home and reconnect with family and friends. When the games were in Wisconsin, Lombardi proudly showed-off the winning tradition that he was building. *Ironically, this winning tradition was built squarely upon the success that Lombardi had against the Giants.* In fact, he was so successful against them that many New Yorkers adopted the attitude of at least we lost to one of our own – a native New Yorker – Go Packers! While it was always difficult for Lombardi not to return to New York to coach the Giants, he honored his contract with Green Bay. In the process, he never had a losing season and his record against the Giants was 4-1.

Vince Lombardi, 1959-67, 98-30-4, 5 NFL Titles

December 31, 1961
NFL Championship Game

GIANTS 0   PACKERS 37
City Stadium, Green Bay, WI

It was Big Ol' New York against Lil' Ol' Green Bay!
Willie Davis

Green Bay shuts out the Giants for the championship and becomes Titletown forever! In the first NFL title championship game ever played in Green Bay, the Packers win their first of five championships with Lombardi.

Though the Giants had the league's best defense in 1961, they could not slowdown the Packers. After the first quarter, the game wasn't close, and Green Bay was perfect the rest of the way. Paul Hornung started the scoring onslaught with a touchdown on the first play of the second quarter. By halftime, the game was virtually over with Green Bay leading 24-0 lead. To rally the offense, the Giants started veteran quarterback Charlie Conerly in the second half. Nothing mattered.

Three Packers were on leave from the Army for the game. Thanks to President Kennedy's help – Lombardi's friend – Paul Hornung was able to play. Along with Boyd Dowler and Ray Nitschke, they dominated the game. Hornung and Dowler scored 25 points in the pounding (19 by Hornung), and a Nitschke interception also led to a touchdown. Green Bay's defense intercepted four passes and held the Giants to six first downs. *It was the first time since 1953 that the Giants were shut out!*

After the game, Y.A. Tittle said, "We couldn't have beaten them if we used 22 men at the same time." With the victory, the Packers go from chumps to champs in just three years. *Titletown and the Lombardi Dynasty are born!*

Giants	0	0	7	7	0
Packers	0	24	10	3	37

GB   Hornung 6yd run (Hornung kick)
GB   Dowler 13yd pass from Starr (Hornung kick)
GB   R. Kramer 14yd pass from Starr (Hornung kick)
GB   Hornung 17yd FG
GB   Hornung 22yd FG
GB   R. Framer 13yd pass from Starr (Hornung kick)
GB   Hornung 19yd FG

1961 NFL Standings

Eastern Division	W	L	T	Pct
New York Giants	*10*	*3*	*1*	*.769*
Philadelphia Eagles	10	4	0	.714
Cleveland Browns	8	5	1	.615
St. Louis Cardinals	7	7	0	.500
Pittsburgh Steelers	6	8	0	.429
Dallas Cowboys	4	9	1	.308
Wash. Redskins	1	12	1	.077

Western Division	W	L	T	Pct
Green Bay Packers	*11*	*3*	*0*	*.786*
Detroit Lions	8	5	1	.615
Baltimore Colts	8	6	0	.571
Chicago Bears	8	6	0	.571
San Francisco 49ers	7	6	1	.538
Los Angeles Rams	4	10	0	.286
Minnesota Vikings	3	11	0	.214

December 30, 1962
NFL Championship Game

PACKERS 16   GIANTS 7
Yankee Stadium, New York, NY

It was Titletown against Tittletown!

The Giants were embarrassed by their performance in the 1961 championship game against the Packers. *They were out for revenge when Lombardi brought the Packers to New York and to Yankee Stadium for the rematch.* The weather though was a bad omen for the Giants (-17 degrees and 40mph winds) and some thought the conditions were worse than the Ice Bowl.

The Packers' defense and the wind grounded Tittle's passing attack. While he threw for 197 yards, several key passes were dropped. *Ray Nitschke's fumble recovery led to the Packers' only touchdown.* Throughout the day, Jim Taylor was engaged in a physical battle with the famed middle linebacker of the Giants Sam Huff. While both were relentless, Taylor scored the game's only touchdown and rushed for 85 brutal yards on 31 carries. Along with Jerry Kramer's three field goals, that was all the Packers needed. After the game, the heroic Taylor was hospitalized with Hepatitis II.

The Packers' defense kept Y.A. Tittle and the Giant offense out of the end zone for the second straight championship game. In two years, the only points the Giants scored against the Packers came from a blocked punt. *Nitschke, the game's MVP, recovered two fumbles and deflected a pass that was intercepted by Dan Currie.*

In 1962, Packers scored the most points in the league, and they gave up the least. They lost just one game. They just might have been the greatest team of the Lombardi Dynasty!

| Packers | 3 | 7 | 3 | 3 | 16 |
| Giants | 0 | 0 | 7 | 0 | 7 |

GB   J. Kramer 26yd FG
GB   Taylor 7yd run (J. Kramer kick)
NY   Collier punt recovery for TD (Chandler kick)
GB   J. Kramer 29yd FG
GB   J. Kramer 30yd FGl

1962 NFL Standings

Eastern Division	W	L	T	Pct
New York Giants	*12*	*2*	*0*	*.857*
Pittsburgh Steelers	9	5	0	.643
Cleveland Browns	7	6	1	.538
Washington Redskins	5	7	2	.417
Dallas Cowboys	5	8	1	.385
St. Louis Cardinals	4	9	1	.308
Philadelphia Eagles	3	10	1	.231

Western Division	W	L	T	Pct.
Green Bay Packers	*13*	*1*	*0*	*.929*
Detroit Lions	11	3	0	.786
Chicago Bears	9	5	0	.643
Baltimore Colts	7	7	0	.500
San Francisco 49ers	6	8	0	.429
Minnesota Vikings	2	11	1	.154
Los Angeles Rams	1	12	1	.077

Ray Nitschke _1958-72_

In 1958, the Packers traded John Martinkovic to the Giants for a third round pick that they used to select Ray Nitschke. Nitschke became the heart and soul of the Packer defense and "...the greatest Packer of all" according to Paul Hornung. One of the most intimidating players of all-time, Nitschke reinvented the middle linebacker position. _He was a seven time all-pro selection and MVP of the1962 Championship Game win over the Giants._ His #66 is one of only five numbers retired by the Packers, and he is a member of the Football Hall of Fame.

Willie Wood _1960-71_

Willie Wood was a tremendous free agent signing by the Packers. _When Wood wasn't drafted out of USC, he contacted the Giants, Packers, 49ers and the Rams for a tryout. Only the Packers responded. He made the team and was tutored by former New York Giant great Emlen Tunnell. Wood was an outstanding safety making the Pro Bowl eight times. His second half interception in Super Bowl I was the turning point of the game._ He is the Packers' all-time punt return leader and second in interceptions. Wood is one of only 13 undrafted free agents in the Football Hall of Fame.

Lionel Aldridge _1964-71_

The Packers traded Paul Dudley to the Giants for a fourth round pick in the 1963 draft. That pick turned out to be Lionel Aldridge. Aldridge was the only rookie ever to start on defense for Lombardi. He was a fine defensive end who played in both of the first two Super Bowls.

December 26, 1965
1965 Western Conference Playoff

COLTS 10 PACKERS 13
Lambeau Field, Green Bay, WI

Had it not been for Chandler and his gifted right foot, there would probably never have been a 1965 NFL title game in Green Bay and what eventually led to an unprecedented three straight league championships by the Packers. Chandler was the lifesaver.
                                        Magnificent Seven

Even though the Packers beat the Colts twice during the 1965 regular season, both teams finished 10-3-1 in the Western Conference. In a sudden-death playoff game ruled by backup quarterbacks, Baltimore was without Johnny Unitas and Gary Cuzzo. Tom Matte, primarily a running back, started in their place. For Green Bay, Bart Starr was hurt on the first play of the game and Zeke Bratkowski led the Packers. *In a defensive battle, Don Chandler's two field goals were the difference. The first forced overtime and the second won the game! Thanks to Chandler, the Packers would return to the title game after a two year absence.*

Colts	7	3	0 0	0	10
Packers	0	0	7 3	3	13

Balt Shinnick 25yd fumble return (Michaels kick)
Balt Michaels 15yd FG
GB Hornung 1yd run (Chandler kick)
GB Chandler 22yd FG
(OT)
GB Chandler 25yd FG

1965 NFL Standings

Eastern Division	W	L	T	Pct
Cleveland Browns	11	3	0	.786
New York Giants	*7*	*7*	*0*	*.500*
Dallas Cowboys	7	7	0	.500
Washington Redskins	6	8	0	.429
Philadelphia Eagles	5	9	0	.357
St. Louis Cardinals	5	9	0	.357
Pittsburgh Steelers	2	12	0	.143

Western Division	W	L	T	Pct.
Green Bay Packers	*10*	*3*	*1*	*.769*
Baltimore Colts	10	3	1	.769
Chicago Bears	9	5	0	.643
San Francisco 49ers	7	6	1	.538
Minnesota Vikings	7	7	0	.500
Detroit Lions	6	7	1	.462
Los Angeles Rams	4	10	0	.286

January 2, 1966
1965 Championship Game

BROWNS 12   PACKERS 23
Lambeau Field, Green Bay, Wis.

The Packers face the defending champion Cleveland Browns for the championship. This was the last NFL championship game before the Super Bowl Era. It was also the last football game for Jim Brown, and the last postseason game for Green Bay's backfield tandem of Paul Hornung and Jim Taylor.

The Packers scored the first time they had the ball on a Bart Starr to Carroll Dale touchdown pass. Cleveland came right back with a touchdown *but missed the extra point thanks to Willie Wood. Wood's second quarter interception also set up a Don Chandler field goal. By halftime, Chandler added another to give Green Bay a 13-12 lead.*

Snow, sleet and rain made the field icy, slippery and muddy! The dreary conditions slowed down Jim Brown, but it did not stop the power of Hornung and Taylor. They led Green Bay to a touchdown to start the second half. This touchdown, a power sweep left by the muddy Hornung, is immortalized by NFL Films.

Green Bay held Cleveland scoreless in the second half. *The key stop was made by Ray Nitschke and Willie Wood who broke up a Frank Ryan pass to Jim Brown in the end zone.* When it was over, Taylor and Hornung combined for over 200 yards rushing while Brown was held to 50. *Don Chandler led all scorers with 11 points, and the Packers won their 9th NFL Championship.*

Browns	9	3	0	0	12
Packers	7	6	7	3	23

GB   Dale 47yd pass from Starr (Chandler kick)
CLE Collins 17yd pass from Ryan (kick failed)
CLE Groza 24yd FG
GB   Chandler 15yd FG
GB   Chandler 23yd FG
CLE Groza 28yd FG
GB   Hornung 13yd run (Chandler kick)
GB   Chandler 29yd FG

Don Chandler   *1965-67*
Babe

Trading a 3rd round draft pick to the Giants for Don Chandler may have been the greatest trade Vince Lombardi ever made. *Not only did Chandler singlehandedly save the 1965 season by beating the Colts in sudden-death overtime, but for three years, Chandler was Mr. Clutch. In seven playoff games, he made 9/12 field goals and 22/23 extra points.* He shares the Super Bowl Record of four field goals in a game, and he still holds the Packers' record for the longest punt (90 yards).

In 1967, Chandler's last season, *he won three games for the Packers and helped lead them to the Ice Bowl and to Vince Lombardi's triumphant finale in Super Bowl II.*

Super Bowls

In June 1966, the battle between the National Football League (NFL) and the American Football League (AFL) officially ended. Beginning with the 1966 season, a championship game would be played between the winners of the two leagues. First, it would be called AFL-NFL World Championship Game, but it quickly became the Super Bowl and Super Bowl Sunday.

Tom Landry

Before there would be Super Bowls for the Packers, there was Tom Landry. *Landry who coached alongside Vince Lombardi with the Giants* was an all-pro defensive back for New York from 1950-1955. He was the leader of the great Giant defenses of the 1950s, and he was one of the game's great defensive innovators as a coach with the 4-3 and the Flex defenses.

But it was Landry's weakness as a player (lack of speed) that led to his greatness as a coach. Since he wasn't exceptionally fast, Landry prepared diligently by studying game film. He knew the tendencies of opposing receivers in every formation. He learned not to "over pursue" which was later the basis for the Flex Defense. From film study, he learned to go the area of the field where he knew the ball was going. He sometimes got there even before the receiver.

Though Lombardi and Landry were different, they remained friends, and they respected each other. Together, they had five straight winning seasons with the Giants (1954-58). They were intelligent and innovative coaches who were leaders in the relatively new art of analyzing game film. The Giants won the 1956 NFL title by crushing Chicago 47-7, and they also played in the 1958 and 1959 NFL championship games.

Uncertain of his future in New York, Lombardi left New York for Green Bay in 1959. Landry left for Dallas the the following season. *Years later, they would meet again as head coaches in two of the NFL's greatest games – the 1966 NFL Championship Game and the "Ice Bowl." In these games, it was Landry's Cowboys who ultimately stood between Vince Lombardi and the Packers' quest for immortality.*

January 1, 1967
1966 NFL Championship Game

PACKERS 34   COWBOYS 27
Cotton Bowl, Dallas, TX

We put in a whole new blocking system for this game.
                                        Vince Lombardi

Lombardi and Landry met to battle for the right to represent the NFL in the first Super Bowl. Both coaches changed plays and formations to keep each other off balance. Lombardi even ran the Packers' power sweep from different formations and in different directions.

Early on, the changes worked and they confused Dallas. The Packers moved the ball easily and jumped out to a 14-0 lead. The Cowboys came back to tie the score at 14, and a high scoring game featuring almost 800 total yards was underway. After a beautiful 51 yard touch-down pass from Bart Starr to Carroll Dale in the second quarter, a Dallas field goal kept it close – 21-17 – at halftime

In the third quarter, another Cowboy field goal cut the lead to 21-20 before Starr struck again for his third and fourth touchdowns of the game. But Don Meredith's 68 yard touchdown to Frank Clarke in the 4th quarter put Dallas within seven. After Green Bay was forced to punt, Dallas took over at the Packer 47 yard line with 2:50 left.

Dallas drove to the Green Bay two yard line. On fourth down, Dave Robinson sacked Meredith as he desperately threw for the end zone. Tom Brown intercepts the pass to seal the victory for Green Bay. The victory gave the Packers back-to-back championships and reservations in Los Angles to represent the NFL in the first Super Bowl.

| Packers | 14 | 7 | 7 | 6 | 34 |
| Cowboys | 14 | 3 | 3 | 7 | 27 |

GB Pitts 17yd pass from Starr (Chandler kick)
GB Grabowski 18yd fumble return (Chandler kick)
Dal Reeves 3yd run (Villanueva kick)
Dal Perkins 23yd run (Villanueva kick)
GB Dale 51yd pass from Starr (Chandler kick)
Dal Villanueva 11 yd FG
Dal Villanueva 32 yd FG
GB Dowler 16yd pass from Starr (Chandler kick)
GB McGee 28yd pass from Starr (kick failed)
Dal Clarke 68yd pass from Meredith (Villanueva kick)

1966 NFL Standings

Eastern Division	W	L	T	Pct
Dallas Cowboys	10	3	1	.769
Cleveland Browns	9	5	0	.643
Philadelphia Eagles	9	5	0	.643
St. Louis Cardinals	8	5	1	.615
Washington Redskins	7	7	0	.500
Pittsburgh Steelers	5	8	1	.385
Atlanta Falcons	3	11	0	.214
New York Giants	*1*	*12*	*1*	*.077*

Western Division	W	L	T	Pct
Green Bay Packers	*12*	*2*	*0*	*.857*
Baltimore Colts	9	5	0	.643
Los Angeles Rams	8	6	0	.571
San Francisco 49ers	6	6	2	.500
Chicago Bears	5	7	2	.417
Detroit Lions	4	9	1	.308
Minnesota Vikings	4	9	1	.308

January 15, 1967
Super Bowl I

CHIEFS 10   PACKERS 35
L.A. Coliseum, Los Angeles, CA

There would be only one *first* Super Bowl, and Vince
Lombardi was determined to win it. He had little regard
for the "new" American Football League (AFL), and he felt
intense pressure from NFL owners and coaches to win the
game for the more established league. The media is
everywhere, and much was expected of the Packers who
were favored by 13.5 points.

The first half was close and well played. The teams
from the rival leagues were competitive. Max McGee's
fantastic touchdown catch, befitting of the first touchdown
in Super Bowl history, gave the Packers the early lead.
The Chiefs countered with a 66 yard touchdown drive
of their own and the Packers led by only four points
at halftime.

During the game, Bart Starr's success on third down gave
the Packers' increasing confidence that they could move
the ball against the Chiefs' secondary. But in the second
half, it was a more aggressive Packer defense that put
Green Bay in control. *On Kansas City's first possession
of the second half, the Packers' unleashed the blitz and
Willie Wood intercepted a Lenny Dawson pass and
returned it 50 yards to the Chiefs' five yard line. On the
next play, Elijah Pitts scored. Wood's play gave Green
Bay the momentum that it would never relinquish.*

The Chiefs gained only 12 total yards in the third quarter.
They ran only four plays in Packer territory during the entire
second half (resulting in two penalties, one sack and one
incomplete pass). The Packers won the biggest game in
pro football history thanks to Max McGee (7 catches for
138 yards and two TDs) and Bart Starr, the game's MVP.

Packers	7	7	14	7	35
Chiefs	0	10	0	0	10

GB McGee 37yd pass from Starr (Chandler kick)
KC McClinton 7yd pass from Dawson (Mercer kick)
GB Taylor 14yd run (Chandler kick)
KC Mercer 31yd FG
GB Pitts 5yd run (Chandler kick)
GB McGee 13yd pass from Starr (Chandler kick)
GB Pitts 1yd run (Chandler kick)

Ray Wietecha *1965-70*
Bob Schnelker *1966-71, 1982-85*

Ray Wietecha and Bob Schnelker both played for
Vince Lombardi when he was an assistant coach
for the Giants. Wietecha was a perennial all-pro center
who never missed a game in his ten year career!
Schnelker was a solid receiver in Lombardi's New York
offense for seven years

*For the Packers, Wietecha was the team's Offensive
Coordinator and Schnelker coached the receivers.
They both coached with Lombardi in Super Bowls I & II.
In the 1980s, Schnelker returned as Green Bay's
Offensive Coordinator.*

December 31, 1967
1967 NFL Championship Game

COWBOYS 17 PACKERS 21
Lambeau Field, Green Bay, WI

…(fans) lit small fires around the stadium to keep warm.
The Ice Bowl

Temperature - 13
Wind Chill - 49

This was the most brutal and memorable game in NFL history. The frozen tundra of Lambeau Field was the stage for Lombardi's last game and the Packers' final struggle for a third straight NFL championship.

Just like last year's title game in Dallas, the Packers jumped ahead 14-0. Boyd Dowler got revenge for Mike Geatcher's vicious hit in the end zone during last year's championship game by grabbing two touchdowns passes from Bart Starr in the first half. The Cowboys then capitalized on two Packer turnovers late in the second quarter to trim the deficit to 14-10 at the half.

In the third quarter, Dallas' defense took control. The Doomsday Defense – which sacked Starr eight times in the game – held the Packers scoreless. The Cowboys then went in front 17-14 on the first play of the fourth quarter. Ironically, they connected on one Lombardi's favorite plays – a half back option pass – that went 50 yards for a touchdown.

With just under five minutes remaining and the Cowboys still in front, *the Packers began their final drive at the 32 after a nine yard punt return by Willie Wood.* The rest of the drive belonged to Starr, Donny Anderson and Chuck Mercein. As the Packers moved downfield, Anderson's number was called seven times for 29 yards. *Mercein's three plays gained 34 yards including a crucial 8 yard run that got the best of Bob Lilly to put the ball at the Dallas three yard line with 54 seconds left.*

After three tries by Anderson that picked up two yards, the Packers called timeout with 16 seconds left. With no timeouts, Lombardi made perhaps the gutsiest call in playoff history. Rather than force overtime with a short field goal, Starr scores on a quarterback sneak and the Packers win. Even the coldest game in NFL history couldn't stop Green Bay's drive for three consecutive NFL championships!

Cowboys	0	10	0	7	17
Packers	7	7	0	7	21

GB Dowler 8yd pass from Starr (Chandler kick)
GB Dowler 43yd pass from Starr (Chandler kick)
DAL Andrie 7yd fumble return (Villanueva kick)
DAL Villanueva 21yd FG
DAL Rentzel 50yd pass from Reeves (Villanueva kick)
GB Starr 1yd run (Chandler kick)

1967 NFL Standings

Century Division	W	L	T	Pct
Cleveland Browns	9	5	0	.643
New York Giants	**7**	**7**	**0**	**.500**
St. Louis Cardinals	6	7	1	.462
Pittsburgh Pirates	4	9	1	.308

Central Division	W	L	T	Pct
Green Bay Packers	**9**	**4**	**1**	**.692**
Chicago Bears	7	6	1	.538
Detroit Lions	5	7	2	.417
Minnesota Vikings	3	8	3	.273

Chuck Mercein   *1967-69*

In November 1967, Lombardi acquired Chuck Mercein from the New York Giants. Mercein, from Wisconsin, was one of the heroes of the Ice Bowl. In the game's final drive, he picked up 34 of the 68 yards to set up the winning touchdown. Packer announcer Ted Moore praised Mercein during that final drive with "Chuck Mercein, the taxi squad refugee, has again proven he was a good acquisition for the Green Bay Packers." The week before the Ice Bowl, *Mercein also scored an important touchdown against the Los Angeles Rams in the Western Conference Championship Game.*

January 14, 1968
Super Bowl II

RAIDERS   14   Green Bay   33
Orange Bowl, Miami, FL

Let's win this one for the old man.

Jerry Kramer

After the Ice Bowl, the Packers went to Florida for the Super Bowl. They practiced at the New York Yankees spring training facility in Fort Lauderdale, and by Super Bowl Sunday, they were ready. It would be the last game of the Lombardi Dynasty.

The Packers were more relaxed and ready for Super Bowl II than they were for the first Super Bowl. They were confident as they took on the younger and less experienced Oakland Raiders. *A slow first half saw three Don Chandler field goals and a Packer touchdown put Green Bay in front 16-7.*

During halftime, several Packer veterans got together

and decided to dedicate the second half to Lombardi. They had heard the retirement rumors, and they had a feeling that this could be his last game. With the defense continuing to pressure Oakland quarterback Daryle Lamonica – Willie Davis had three sacks – the offense quickly got in gear.

On the second drive of the third quarter, the Packers marched 82 yards for a touchdown. The drive was kept alive by another clutch catch by Max McGee. On a classic third and one call from the Green Bay 40 yard line, Starr's play-action pass to McGee netted 35 yards. The play completes McGee's Super Bowl legacy and the Packers score seven plays later to go up 23-7.

In the fourth quarter, Herb Adderley's 60 yard pass interception for a touchdown put the game away for Green Bay. *Don Chandler set a Super Bowl record with four field goals, and he led all scorers with 15 points. Along with Lombardi, he would go out on top and retire after Super Bowl II.*

Packers	3	13	10	7	33
Raiders	0	7	0	7	14

GB   Chandler 39yd FG
GB   Chandler 20yd FG
GB   Dowler 62yd pass from Starr (Chandler kick)
OAK Miller 23yd pass from Lamonica (Blanda kick)
GB   Chandler 43yd FG
GB   Anderson 2yd run (Chandler kick)
GB   Chandler 31yd FG
GB   Adderley 60yd interception return (Chandler kick)
OAK Miller 23yd pass from Lamonica (Blanda kick)

Frank Winters   _1992-2002_
Baggadonuts

Frank Winters played for the Green Bay Packers after stints with the Browns, Giants (1989) and Chiefs. He was the Packers' starting center from 1992-2002 and he anchored Green Bay's offensive line in two Super Bowls. Winters was inducted into the Packer Hall of Fame in 2008.

January 20, 2008
NFC Championship Game

GIANTS   23   Packers   20
Lambeau Field, Green Bay, WI

We can't make the short one, but we make the 47 yarder in overtime to make it exciting.
> _Lawrence Tynes_

This was the third coldest game in NFL history with a game time temperature of -1 and a wind chill of -23 degrees.

For a berth in the Super Bowl, the Giants had the Herculean task of facing Brett Favre and the Packers on the frozen tundra of Lambeau Field. The Packers had also beaten the Giants earlier in the year, and 2007 was looking magical for Brett Favre and the Packers.

Two field goals put New York up early, but the Packers struck suddenly with a record-setting 90 yard touchdown pass from Favre to Donald Driver. It put Green Bay in front 7-6, and the Packers led at halftime 10-6. But as conditions worsened in the third quarter, it surprisingly took more of a toll on Favre and the Packers than on the Giants. In absolute frigid conditions, the Giants physical front seven began to dominate. The Packers mustered only 28 yards rushing all game, while the Giants' Brandon Jacobs and Ahmad Bradshaw pounded Green Bay for 130 yards. And although Eli Manning's connection with Plaxico Burress was nearly unstoppable – 11 catches for 154 yards – the game stood deadlocked at 20 early in the fourth quarter.

After Lawrence Tynes missed a 36 yard field goal attempt at the end of regulation, the teams went into overtime. The Packers won the toss. On the second play of overtime, Favre's pass to Driver was intercepted by Corey Webster. Four plays later the Giants were on their way to Super Bowl XLVI and their historic win over the undefeated New England Patriots!

This was Brett Favre's last game as a Packer and the last of his 8,758 passes for the Green & Gold.

Giants	3	3	14	0	3	23
Packers	0	10	7	3	0	20

NY   Tynes FG 29
NY   Tynes FG 37
GB   Driver 90yd pass from Favre (Crosby kick)
GB   Crosby FG 36
NY   Jacobs 1yd run (Tynes kick)
GB   Lee 12yd pass from Favre (Crosby kick)
NY   Bradshaw 4yd run (Tynes kick)
GB   Cosby FG 37
OT
NY   Tynes FG

2007 NFL Standings

NFC East	W	L	T	Pct.
Dallas Cowboys	13	3	0	.813
New York Giants	10	6	0	.625
Washington Redskins	9	7	0	.563
Philadelphia Eagles	8	8	0	.500

NFC North	W	L	T	Pct.
Green Bay Packers	13	3	0	.813
Minnesota Vikings	8	8	0	.500
Chicago Bears	7	9	0	.438
Detroit Lions	7	9	0	.438

Ryan Grant 2007-2011

Grant was acquired from the Giants in 2007 for a 6th round draft pick. He was Green Bay's leading rusher for three straight seasons before injuries temporarily derailed his career. He holds the Packer record for rushing yards in a playoff game - 201 yards vs. Seattle in the 2007 Divisional Round. In the conference championship game loss to the Giants, Grant forced the fumble that led to Mason Crosby's game tying field goal with 11:46 left in regulation.

December 26, 2010

GIANTS 17   PACKERS 45
Lambeau Field, Green Bay, WI

…the proud New York Giants were swept right off their feet.

This was a de Facto playoff game with the loser going home for the postseason. The Giants came into Lambeau with the confidence of 2007, but the Packers had Aaron Rodgers back from a concussion he suffered two weeks earlier.

The game was close in the first half. The Packers jumped
ahead with an 80 yard pass from Rodgers to Jordy Nelson.
They pushed it to 14-0 before Eli Manning connected with
Hakeem Nicks and Mario Manningham to even it at 14.
John Kuhn then scored the first of his three touchdowns
to put the Packers back in front.

Green Bay poured it on in the second half. Manning was
intercepted three times. Two were returned for touchdowns.
The Packers controlled the Giants' running game by holding
Ahmad Bradshaw and Brandon Jacobs to 78 yards. But the
game belonged to Rodgers who threw for 404 yards and four
touchdowns. *The offense generated 515 yards, the most given
up by the Giants in 30 years.*

This victory over the Giants begins the longest winning streak
in Green Bay Packer history! The team was an offensive
jauggernaut, and their 19 game winning streak included a
Super Bowl XLV victory over the Pittsburgh Steelers.

Giants	0	14	3	0	17
Packers	14	7	10	14	45

GB   Nelson 80yd pass from Rodgers (Crosby kick)
GB   Jones 3yd pass from Rodgers (Crosby kick)
NY   Nicks 36yd pass from Manning (Tynes kick)
NY   Manningham 85yd pass from Manning (Tynes kick)
GB   Kuhn 8yd run (Crosby kick)
GB   Crosby 31yd FG
NY   Tynes 38yd FG
GB   Lee 1yd pass from Rodgers (Crosby kick)
GB   Kuhn 5yd pass from Rodgers (Crosby kick)
GB   Kuhn 1yd run (Crosby kick)

2010 NFL Standings

NFC East	W	L	T	Pct.
Philadelphia Eagles	10	6	0	.625
New York Giants	10	6	0	.625
Washington Redskins	6	10	0	.375
Dallas Cowboys	6	10	0	.375
NFC North	W	L	T	Pct.
Chicago Bears	11	5	0	.688
Green Bay Packers	10	6	0	.625
Minnesota Vikings	6	10	0	.375
Detroit Lions	6	10	0	.375

Charlie Peprah *2006-08, 2010-11*

Charlie Peprah was claimed off waivers from the Giants in 2006. He played on special teams and as the backup safety until 2010 when he replaced an injured Morgan Burnett and started 11 games on the way to Super Bowl XLV. Peprah had a key second half interception in the NFC Championship Game win against the Bears. In 2011, he stepped-in again for the injured Nick Collins.

January 15, 2012
NFC Divisional Playoff

GIANTS 37   PACKERS 20
Lambeau Field, Green Bay, WI

Four years after their historic victory over the Packers in the NFC Championship Game, the Giants return to Lambeau in the post-season. They return riding a three game winning streak that included a first round playoff win over Atlanta. After a first round bye in the playoffs, the 15-1 Packers await the Giants. While the pre-game publicity focused on the similarities between this game and the 2007 NFC Conference Championship Game, this time the game was no contest. With their defense unable to pressure Manning, he shredded the Packer defense in the air and on the ground for 420 total yards. His precision passing and third down efficiency kept drives alive. Hakeem Nicks was his primary target with seven catches for 165 yards and two touchdowns. The ultimate insult came just before halftime when he caught a 37 yard *Hail Mary* pass to extend the Giants' lead to 20-10.

Throughout the game, Green Bay was inconsistent on both sides of the ball. Aaron Rodgers was the team's leading rusher (66 yards) and the Packers turned the ball over four times.

Plain and simple, the Giants crushed and embarrassed the Packers. Green Bay's defense "...ceded large chunks of real estate...running backs put the ball on the ground... and receivers dropped passes...". From start to finish, the Giants dominated Green Bay and the mystique of Lambeau Field no longer seems to apply to the Giants, especially in the postseason.

Giants	10	10	0	17	37
Packers	3	7	3	7	20

NY   Tynes 31yd FG
GB   Crosby 47 FG
NY   Nicks 66yd pass from Manning (Tynes kick)
GB   Kuhn 8yd pass from Rodgers (Crosby kick)
NY   Tynes 23yd FG
NY   Nicks 37yd pass from Manning (Tynes kick)
GB   Crosby 35yd FG
NY   Tynes 35-yard FG
NY   Manningham 4yd pass from Manning (Tynes kick)
GB   Driver 16yd pass from Rodgers (Crosby kick)
NY   Brandon Jacobs 14yd run (Tynes kick)

2011 NFL Standings

NFC East	W	L	T	Pct.
New York Giants	9	7	0	.563
Philadelphia Eagles	8	8	0	.500
Dallas Cowboys	8	8	0	.500
Washington Redskins	5	11	0	.313

NFC North	W	L	T	Pct.
Green Bay Packers	15	1	0	.938
Detroit Lions	10	6	0	.625
Chicago Bears	8	8	0	.500
Minnesota Vikings	3	13	0	.188

Jimmy Robinson   *2006-10*

In 2006, Jimmy Robinson joined Mike McCarthy's first staff in Green Bay. Robinson had a successful career as a receiver for the New York Giants (1976-79). He also coached for the Giants before coming to Green Bay. *Robinson coached receivers, and he developed a very talented group: Greg Jennings, Jordy Nelson, Jermichael Finley, James Jones and Donald Driver. With Aaron Rodgers, they led the Packers to victory in Super Bowl XLV.*

Conclusion

While Green Bay, Wisconsin and New York City are polar opposites, they share a unmatched legacy of football greatness. The Packers and the Giants have appeared in more NFL championship games than any other two teams. They have each enjoyed dominant eras when they have set the standard for both winning and innovation for the rest of the league.

Since 1928, they have played each other 57 times. Green Bay holds a 31-24-2 edge. With the Giants turning the tables recently with two straight postseason victories at Lambeau, the rivalry is being stoked once again. But after 84 years, the Giant – Packer connection has been been particularly sweet for the Giant Cheeseheads who found greatness in the small city in Northeastern Wisconsin!

EXTRA CHEESE!

October 1, 1933   **NY 10**   **GB 7**
Green Bay's first game in Milwaukee is against the
Giants. It's played at Borchert Field, an old wooden
baseball park on Milwaukee's north side. Support
from Milwaukee is crucial to the Packers' survival
in Green Bay.

November 17, 1940   **NY 7**   **GB 3**
The Packers are the first pro football team to travel by
plane to a game. After refueling in Cleveland, poor
weather in New York cancels the flight. The Packers
took the train the rest of the way.

August 23, 1941   **NY 17**   **GB 17**
In a preseason game, Larry Craig of the Packers and
Hank Soar of the Giants were the first players fined by
the NFL – $25.00 each – for fighting.

November 21, 1948   **NY 49**   **GB 3**
Green Bay's worst loss in the 1940s.

September 4, 1961   **GB 20**   **NY 17**
The first Bishop's Charities Game (preseason) was started
by Lombardi to support the Catholic Diocese of Green Bay.
The first five games are against the Giants, and the
Packers win all five.

December 3, 1961   **GB 20**   **NY 17**
Packers beat the Giants in Milwaukee to clinch the
Western Division. It is Lombardi's first win over the
Giants.

October 22, 1967   **GB 48**   **NY 21**
Bart Starr's first touchdown pass of the season finally
gets Green Bay rolling toward their second Super Bowl title.

September 19, 1971   **GB 42**   **NY 40**
In his first game as coach, Dan Devine's leg is broken in a sideline pile-up.

September 20, 1982   **GB 27**   **NY 19**
The Packers and Giants play the last football game before the 1982 strike. The strike stops play for two months.

January 6, 2002   **GB 34**   **NY 25**
New York's Michael Strahan sacks Brett Favre to set the single season sack record with 22.5 sacks.

September 16, 2007   **GB 35**   **NY 13**
Brett Favre's 149th career win. He passes Elway for most wins by an NFL quarterback.

December 4, 2011   **GB 38**   **NY 35**
A field goal by Mason Crosby with three seconds left wins it. The Packers' undefeated streak that began in 2010 against the Giants reaches 17.

GIANT CHEESEHEADS ROSTER

	GIANTS →	PACKERS
Cal Hubbard, T	1927-28, 1936	1929-33, 1935
Mule Wilson, RB	1927-30	1930-31
Dick Stahlman, T	1927, 1930	1931-32
"Red" Smith, QB, coach	1928, 1931	1927, 1929
Rudy Comstock, G	1930	1931-33
Bo Molenda, RB, coach	1932-35, 1936-41	1928-32, 1947-48
Arnie Herber, QB	1944-45	1930-40
Clarke Hinkle, RB		1932-41
Emlen Tunnell, DB	1948-58	1959-1961
Bill Austin, G/C, coach	1949-57	1959-1965
Tom Landry, DB, coach	1950-55	
Ray Weitecha, C, coach	1953-62	1965-70
Vince Lombardi, coach	1954-58	1959-1968
Bob Schnelker, TE, coach	1954-60	1965-71
Don Chandler, K	1956-64	1965-67
Ray Nitschke, LB		1958-72
Willie Wood, S		1960-71
Lionel Aldridge, DE		1963-71
Chuck Mercein, RB	1965-67	1967-69
Frank Winters, C	1989	1992-2002
Jimmy Robinson, WR, coach	1976-79,1998-03	2006-2010
Charlie Peprah, DB		2006-08, 2010-11
Ryan Grant, RB		2007-11
"Dutch" Webber, E	1926 →	1928
Elbert Bloodgood, RB, K	1928	1930
Tom Potsy Jones, G	1932-36	1938
Lee Mulleaneaux, C	1932	1938
Ward Cuff, RB, K	1937-45	1947
Steve Pritko, E	1943	1949-50
Ben Agajanian, K	1949, 1950-57	1961
Ben Davidson, DE	1961	1961
Francis Peay, T	1966-67	1968-72
Randy Johnson, QB	1971-73	1976
Dave Roller, DT	1971	1975-78
Dick Enderle, G	1972-75	1976
Ray Rhodes, DB, WR, Coach	1974-79	1992-93, 1999
Lindy Infante, Coach	1977-78	1988-91
Billy Ard, G/T	1981-88	1989-91
Bill Neill, NT	1981-83	1984
Phil McConkey, WR	1984-85, 1986-88	1986

Sean Landetta, P	1985-93, 2006	1998
Mark Collins, DB	1986-93	1997
Adrian White, S	1987-91	1992
Mark Ingram, WR	1987-92	1995
Frank Winters, C	1989	1992-2002
Keith Crawford, DB, WR	1993	1995, 1999
Frank Walker, DB	2003-06	2007
Kenderick Allen, DT	2004-05	2006

GIANTS ← PACKERS

Dutch Hendrian, K, RB	1925	1924
Tillie Voss, E	1926	1924
Roman R. Rosatti, T	1928	1924, 1926-27
Jim Bowdoin, G	1932	1928-32
Jesse Quatse, T	1935	1933
Ken Keuper, RB	1948	1945-47
Ray Pelfrey, E	1953	1951-52
Jack Spinks, G	1956-57	1955-56
John Martinkovic, DE	1957	1951-56
Al Barry, G	1958-59	1954, 1957
Dick Pesonen, DB	1962-64	1960
John McDowell, G	1965	1964
Allen Jacobs, RB	1966-67	1965
Dave Hathcock, DB	1967	1966
Steve Wright, T	1968-69	1964-67
Tommy Crutcher, LB	1968-69	1964-67, 1971-72
Dave Dunaway, WR	1969	1968
Junior Coffey, RB	1969, 1970	1965
Bob Hyland, C	1971-75	1967-69, 76
Carl Wafer, DT	1974	1974
Mike McCoy, DT	1979-80	1970-76
Steve Odom, WR, KR	1979	1974-79
Jim Culbeath, RB	1980	1977-79
Joe McLaughlin, LB	1980-84	1979
Tim Stokes, T	1981	1978-82
Casey Merrill, DE	1983-86	1979-83
Tom Coughlin, Coach	1988-90, 2004 -	1986-87
Tom Flynn, S	1986-88	1984-86
Joe Prokop, P	1992	1985
Brett Conway, K	2003	1997
Terrell Buckley, DB	2005	1992-94
Grey Ruegamer, C/G	2006-08	2003-05
Dave Tollefson, DT	2007-11	2006

Giants vs. Packers 1928-2011

Date	Score	Location, Attendance & Headlines		
10 7 28	Giants 6-0	GB	9,000	Triple pass wins game!
11 18 28	Packers 7-0	NY	---	
11 24 29	Packers 20-6	NY	25,000	GB's victory clinches title
10 5 30	Packers 14-7	GB	11,000	55yd pass to Blood wins it
11 23 30	Giants 13-6	NY		Army's Chris Cagle debuts
10 4 31	Packers 27-7	GB	14,000	
11 22 31	Packers 14-10	NY	40,000	Friedman sacked!
10 2 32	Packers 13-0	GB		
11 20 32	Giants 6-0	NY		GB's first loss of the year
10 1 33	Giants 10-7	Milw	13,000	First game in Milwaukee
11 26 33	Giants 17-6	NY		
9 30 34	Packers 20-6	Milw	11,000	
11 11 34	Giants 17-3	NY		Two NY TDs by Newman
9 29 35	Packers 16-7	GB		Hubbard interception TD
11 22 36	Packers 26-14	NY	20,000	
11 21 37	Giants 10-0	NY	38,965	
11 20 38	Giants 15-3	NY	48,279	5 interceptions by NY
12 11 38	**Giants 23-17**	**NY**	**48,120**	**Danowski's = NY hero!**
12 10 39	**Packers 27-0**	**Milw**	**32,279**	**GB's 5th NFL Title**
11 17 40	Giants 7-3	NY	28,262	Kickoff dooms GB
11 22 42	Tie 21-21	NY	30,246	
10 31 43	Packers 35-21	NY		2 Canadeo TDs keys
11 19 44	Giants 24-0	NY		NY defense dominates
12 17 44	**Packers 14-7**	**NY**	**46,016**	**WI native Fritsch stars!**
11 25 45	Packers 23-14	NY	52,681	Brock stars for GB defense
11 23 47	Tie 24-24	NY	27,939	
11 21 48	Giants 49-3	Milw	12,639	
11 13 49	Giants 30-10	GB	20,151	Conerly throws for 4 TDs!
11 16 52	Packers 17-3	NY	26,723	
11 3 57	Giants 31-17	GB	32,070	Tunnell's 52yd interception!
11 1 59	Giants 20-3	NY	68,837	
12 3 61	Packers 20-17	Milw	47,012	GB clinches conference
12 31 61	**Packers 37-0**	**GB**	**39,029**	**Titletown!**
12 30 62	**Packers 16-7**	**NY**	**64,892**	**Repeat!**
10 22 67	Packers 48-21	NY	62,585	
11 30 69	Packers 20-10	Milw	48,156	

Date	Score	Location, Attendance & Headlines		
9 19 71	Giants 42-40	GB	56,263	Seven Packer turnovers!
10 7 73	Packers 16-14	NH	70,050	
11 23 75	Packers 40-14	Milw	50,150	
11 16 80	Giants 27-21	NY	72,368	
10 4 81	Packers 27-14	NY	71,684	
11 8 81	Packers 26-24	Milw	54,138	
9 20 82	Packers 27-19	NY	68,405	A win before the strike
9 26 83	Giants 27-3	NY	75,308	Monday Night Blowout!
9 15 85	Packers 23-20	GB	56,149	
12 20 86	Giants 55-24	NY	71,351	
12 19 87	Giants 20-10	NY	51,013	
11 8 92	Giants 27-7	NY	72,038	
9 17 95	Packers 14-6	GB	60,117	
11 15 98	Packers 37-3	NY	76,272	GB outgains NY by 300+
1 6 02	Packers 34-25	NY	78,601	
10 3 04	Giants 14-7	GB	70,623	
9 16 07	Packers 35-13	NY	78,701	
1 20 08	Giants 23-20	GB	72,740	Giants to Super Bowl!
12 26 10	Packers 45-17	GB	70,649	
12 4 11	Packers 38-35	NY	80,634	
1 15 12	Giants 37-20	GB	72,080	Giants again!

Packers lead series   31-24-2

Works Cited

10/8/28
New York Times, October 8, 1928

11/24/29
Passing Game: Benny Friedman and the Transformation of Football, p. 200, Greenburg, 2008
Curly Lambeau: The Man Behind the Mystique, p.84, Zimmerman, 2003
Green Bay Press Gazette, November 25, 1929

11/23/30
Passing Game: Benny Friedman and the Transformation of Football, p. 209, Greenberg, 2008

11/22/31
Green Bay Press Gazette, November 23, 1931

Modern NFL
Packers vs. Bears, p. 55, Swain, 1996

12/13/36
New York Daily News, Jack Miley, December 14, 1936
Green Bay Press Gazette, George Calhoun, December 14, 1936

12/11/38
New York Times, Arthur Daley, December 12, 1938
New York Daily News, Jack Mahon, December 12, 1938

Clarke Hinkle
The Packer Legend: An Inside Look, p.57, Torinus, 1982

12/10/39
Green Bay Press Gazette, Dick Flatley, December 11, 1939
Green Bay Packers: Measure of Greatness, p. 395, Goska, 2004
Green Bay Press Gazette, John Walter, December 11, 1939
Green Bay Press Gazette Headline, December 11, 1939

Arnie Herber
Clark Shaughnessy

12/17/44
New York Times, William Anderson, December 18, 1944

Red Smith
The History of the Green Bay Packers, Vol.2, p. 219, Larry
Names, 1987

12/31/61
Lombardi, p. 118 John Wiebusch, 1971
Sport World Magazine, p.46, 12/67

Ray Nitschke
Golden Boy, p. 86, Paul Hornung

12/26/65
Magnificent Seven, p. 53 Bud Lea, 2002

1/1/67
Greatest Moments in Green Bay Packers Football History,
p. 75, Korth, 1998

12/31/67
The Ice Bowl, p. 22, Ed Gruver, 1998

Chuck Mercein
The Ice Bowl, p. 195, Ed Guver, 1998

1/20/08
New York Times, Pat Borzi, January 21, 2008

12/26/10
The Pack is Back! Collector's Edition, p. 73, McGinn, KCI

1/15/12
jsonline.com, Gary D'Amato, January 15, 2012

Bibliography

Black & Blue, Berghaus, 2007
Cowboys Have Always Been My Heroes, Golenbock, 1997
Curly Lambeau: The Man Behind the Mystique, Zimmerman, 2003
Giants Among Men, Cavanaugh, 2008
Golden Boy, Reed, 2004
Greatest Moments in Green Bay Packer Football History, Korth,1998
Green Bay Packers: Measure of Greatness, Goska, 2003
Green Bay Packers 2010 Media Guide
Green Bay Packers: Trials, Triumphs and Tradition, Povletich, 2012
Lombardi, Wiebusch, 1971
Lombardi & Landry, Palladino, 2011
Magnificent Seven, Lea, 2002
Mudbaths & Bloodbaths, D'Amato & Christl, 1997
New York Giants: 75 Years, Daily News, 1999
New York Giants: The Complete Illustrated History, Freedman, 2009
Packers by the Numbers, Maxymuk, 2003
Packers vs. Bears, Swain, 1996
Passing Game, Greenberg, 2008
Pro Football, Cope, 1974
Sunday's Heroes, Whittingham, 2003
The Game That Was, Cope, 1974
The History of the Green Bay Packers, Vol 1-3, Names, 1987
The Ice Bowl, Gruver, 1998
The Illustrated History of the New York Giants, Wittingham, 2005
The Packer Legend, Torinus, 1982
The Scrapbook History of G.B. Packers Football, Zimmerman, 2006
This Day in Green Bay Packer History, Everson, 1998
Titletown's Team: A Photographic History, G.B. Press Gazette, 2009
Vagabond Halfback, Gullickson, 2006
Vince: A Personal Biography of Vince Lombardi, O'Brien, 1987
When Pride Still Mattered, Maraniss, 1999

13799583R00039

Made in the USA
Charleston, SC
01 August 2012